For my Dad.
The best poet I ever knew.

Motherhood
For Slackers
Poems and Prose

Emma Robinson

CONTENTS

ACKNOWLEDGMENTS

Many people say that 'Facebook Friends' aren't real friends. As my Facebook friends have been the ones to encourage, support and publicise me, I beg to differ. Thank you for every Like, Comment and Share. You keep me going.

Thank you to my mum – my best friend, childcare provider and chief publicist.

Thank you to my beautiful, crazy children who give me something to write about.

And lastly, thank you to my very funny and long suffering husband. Without whom, this Slacker Mum wouldn't achieve anything.

Nine Months

I've been taking Folic Acid
and stopped drinking any wine.
Your dad thinks it's his birthday
(we do 'it' all the time.)
But little do I know yet,
the job's already done.
We've started our nine month journey
and this has been month one.

Month Two, the test results are in
but so's the morning sickness.
I'm desperate already to see a bump,
but there's just a little thickness.
You're our little secret just for now,
a glint in Daddy's eye.
Although I want to burst out loud
and tell every passer-by.

Month Three and we can see you
in fuzzy black and white.
Our excitement is a cliché;
we show everyone in sight.
"There's its tiny nose," we point.
"How lovely," they all said.
You've tiny fingers, tiny toes
(and a rather massive head.)

Month Four and now I don't feel sick
and start to have some cravings.
Which consist of any type of food
if covered in chocolate shavings.
Then it's time for a special moment
that truly fills me up with joy.
When I listen to your heartbeat
on the midwife's clever toy.

Month Five and it's time for another scan -
the cold gel makes me chilly.
Everyone is staring hard
to see if there's a willy.
We don't know if you're boy or girl,
so nothing pink or blue.
White babygros, white vests, white hats
and tiny yellow shoes.

Month Six: we're in the final stage
and start to look for a pram.
Your dad is heard to mumble:
"These cost more than my first van."
This month's when I first feel you,
small movements in my tummy.
And suddenly it feels so real
I'm going to be a mummy . . .

Month Seven and my clothes don't fit,
so I browse maternity collections.
Knickers you could camp in
and jeans with extra sections.
People say I'm 'blooming';
pat my ever-expanding tum.
(I know that you need padding
but why's it on my bum?)

Month Eight I start to waddle
and I find it hard to bend.
I'm weeing like a racehorse
and I'm eating like his friend.
And if you've seen a beetle writhe
when turned upon his back;
You've got an idea of how I look
when getting out the sack.

Month Nine and I am desperate.
This waiting game's a 'mare.
Attempting any old wives' tales
to get you out of there.
I'm fat and tired and impatient
with chronic indigestion.
I've tried pineapple and raspberry leaf
(but not the other suggestion.)

Month Nine plus one and I feel a twinge
that's not a Braxton Hick.
I take a bath, switch on the TENS
and get your dad home quick.
I'm scared, excited, happy,
terrified and over the moon.
And suddenly it dawns on me,
I'll get to meet you soon.

The longest nine months of my life
and somehow I've survived.
The moment I've dreaded and longed for
has finally arrived.
And I try to take a moment
despite the cramp and coming pain.
Because one thing is for certain,
life will never be the same.

Letter to my pregnant self.

You are going to have a C-Section. Yes, I know you believe you have a strong pain threshold, you've been to all the birth prep classes and read all the books. It doesn't matter. This child (I won't spoil the surprise and tell you the sex) is going to get stuck and there's nothing you can do about it. Don't let anyone make you feel bad about it. Some women (yes, I know we're supposed to support one another but some girls didn't get that memo) will enjoy telling you how they managed the whole thing with the merest whiff of gas and air and that some women 'make a fuss' or 'didn't try hard enough'. I repeat: your baby will get STUCK, there is NOTHING you can do about it. Don't get angry with these women, don't come home and cry because you didn't have a 'real' birth; smile sweetly, walk away and pray that karma will ensure they get horrendous teenagers.

(Incidentally, these are usually the same mothers who will tell you that their child slept through the night at two weeks old, ate a full roast dinner with a knife and fork at six months and was sitting on a potty, reading The Guardian, weeks before their second birthday. The advice above continues to apply.)

Your child will not sleep alone for a whole night for a long long time. Give in to it, you will get more sleep if you do and life will be a lot easier. Don't spend all that money on 'How to get your child to sleep' books - you won't stick to their advice and you're better off spending the money on expensive make up to cover the bags under your eyes. You will want to kill anyone who tells you that their child puts themselves to sleep, stays that way all night and doesn't rise 'til 8am. Just wait it out, often their second child is not the same. Then you can make supportive noises whilst internally laughing your head off. Eventually your child will choose to sleep in their own bed and not end up in yours by 2am. Surprisingly, you will miss it.

Breast feeding proves to be much trickier to get the hang of than you think it's going to be. You might want to start rubbing your nipples with sandpaper now in preparation. It does get better and eventually becomes pretty great. You will have friends who try to breastfeed and find it doesn't work out for them. Be extra kind to them; they often feel crappy about it, and you need to balance out the judgement they feel from the super mothers.

You are not going to write a novel whilst you're on maternity leave. I know you think you will have lots of time but what you don't know yet is that babies eat time when you're not looking. Your husband will ask you what you've done all day and you will only be able to remember two hours worth of activities. The rest of the day has been eaten by the baby. Don't stress: the novel will happen one day.

Nothing I can say now will prepare you for how you are going to feel about this small person. Remember when you first fell in love and couldn't bear to be away from that boy for a second? Multiply that feeling by 100 and you're getting close. That doesn't mean you won't also feel exasperated, overwhelmed, emotional, angry, frustrated, isolated, terrified and exhausted (sometimes all within the same two hours.) It just means that, when they are asleep in your arms, you will look down and feel a passionate love that you could never have imagined.

In summary, I know that this is something which we don't like to admit, but in the coming weeks and months, you will need to accept that you are often going to be wrong.

Firstly, you will think you couldn't possibly be any more tired. You will be.

Often, you will feel overwhelmed and think you can't do this. You can.

Sometimes, you will think you are the only one who finds it difficult. You are not.

Lastly, you will look at that tiny creature and think that you could never love another human being as much as you love that baby.

And then you will have another one.

First night

The ward is all quiet now
The lights are down low
The visitors and daddies have all had to go

The mothers are resting
Their babies asleep
One nurse at the station, a watch she will keep

We've had quite a journey
Intense and unreal
I've felt things I never expected to feel

Moments of excitement
Moments of panic
An ending not planned and incredibly frantic

But now it's all over
It's just you and I
I knew you the moment you gave that first cry

I look at you sleeping
So still and so small
I am your mummy and you are my all.

Weaning by Limerick

We started six months on the dot

Homemade puree in small coloured pots

The 'aeroplane' hovered

We needn't have bothered

You grimaced and spat out the lot

'You must persevere' we were told

'Maybe the food is too cold?'

We made the slop warmer

(we even tried korma)

Your appetite wasn't cajoled

'Try Baby Led Weaning' they said

So we gave you the food whole instead

Broccoli and carrot sticks

Picked up and given flicks

Then thrown back over your head

The clinic said 'Just keep on trying'

Looked at us as if we were lying

But meals were so stressy

And increasingly messy

All ending with one of us crying

We were at the end of our rope

With mealtimes we just couldn't cope

Then one day those lips parted

Your eating had started

And just when we'd given up hope!

It's all gone to pot(ty). . .

When we potty trained our son two years ago, we prepared physically, mentally and spiritually.

We borrowed the Gina Ford Potty Training book from a friend (after the small fortune spent on useless books about sleep I now borrow rather than buy childcare books), bought an upstairs and a downstairs potty for the house and one for the car, waited for a week where we had a clear social diary and embarked upon Mission Potty Training.

This time around, with our daughter, it was more, "Bugger. We've run out of nappies. Shall we just do it?"

To be honest, she has been ready for potty training for months. The 'experts' tell you there are certain signs that a child is ready to be successfully potty trained: ability to follow instructions, ability to take their own pants down, ability to communicate that they need to use the toilet. When I tell you that she chooses and puts on her own clothes, orders for herself when we eat out and lays out a nappy, wipes and cream before laying herself on a changing mat, you may question who it is in this scenario that is not ready for potty training.

There is one reason and one reason only. This time, I know what I'm letting myself in for.

Nappies are so easy. With nappies, you don't need a GPS reference for your three closest toilets. Although obviously you try to change a nappy as soon as it is necessary, you have more time to find somewhere to do it. Changing nappies isn't pleasant, and they're unhealthy for the environment and your bank balance, but they *are* the devil you know.

Day three of potty training and I needed to go to the shops to buy a birthday card. Slightly bored by her mother's perusal of the shelves, the girl decides she needs to go to the toilet. Right now.

Cue panic stricken mother: ignoring queues of people to demand the shop assistant tell me whether they have a customer toilet (which of course they don't, although I hear them being very sorry as I hot foot it from the store.); running at break neck speed to Debenhams because they have a toilet; waiting an interminably long time for the lift to come; dashing into the toilet; wrestling the potty out of the bag; yanking knickers down; putting the child on the potty. Then . . .

Nothing. Not a trickle. "No mummy, it won't come."

It takes every ounce of patience that I possess (not a very deep well to begin with) not to scream, "But you said you were desperate!"

Then begins the debate. "Just sit there until it does come."

"But it won't come."

"Just try. Squeeze."

(Pathetic squeezing noise.) "No, it won't come."

Eventually, I give in. Knickers back up, potty back under the buggy, hands washed. We go back down in the lift, back to our original shop and, yep, you've guessed it.

After the third unproductive trip to the toilet, I seriously begin to consider whipping out the potty in the middle of the shopping centre and accepting the disgusted looks from the more civilised people walking past. (*I understand*, I want to tell them, *I was you once*.) I am only prevented from doing so by the realisation that I would then need to dispose of the contents somehow.

As I'm sure you can understand, this kind of erratic behaviour is not my idea of a good time.

However, when she does manage to perform the requested task, her delight in her own achievement is infectious. I tell her that she is a good girl, that mummy is very proud and. as I watch her twirling around, proud in equal measure of her new abilities and her Minnie Mouse knick-knacks, I realise that a baby without a nappy isn't actually a baby anymore. She is, in her own words, "a big girl now."

And maybe that's the real reason I've been putting it off.

The Mum Olympics

Seen games for World and Commonwealth
and all the many others?
Now join us for an Olympics which is 'specially for mothers.

First we have the sprint event
Mum and trolley on the blocks.
In under 15 minutes, they must do the weekly shop.

Then the middle distance run
will start with a loud hooter.
As the mothers chase a three year old let loose upon his scooter.

The throwing events have been replaced
with catching skills instead.
So, a discus full of dinner will be launched at mummy's head.

The high jump's always popular
(as all children would expect)
because mums across the country threaten they'll be for it next.

Now get behind this mummy
I want to hear you bellow.
As she breaks the long jump record across a room that's spread with
Lego.

 If it rains, please go inside
and watch the wrestling mums.
Trying to change the nappies of some very wriggly bums.

The weight events are also there
How much is that woman lifting?
Bags and toys and a two year old, from hip to hip she's shifting.

That ends today's Olympics,
but don't be filled with sorrow.
Most mums do these things every day, so just come back tomorrow!

Long Car Journeys

I have idyllic, probably rose-tinted, memories of long car journeys to Cornwall as a child. Being carried from my bed, half asleep, wrapped in a sleeping bag. Snuggled under a blanket in the back seat with my younger sister, eating car sweets, playing eye spy, singing along to my dad's Beatles tapes and dozing off again, before waking up six hours later parked up at a Cornish beach. My husband has similar memories of holiday trips to Wales and recreating these journeys was something we looked forward to with our own children, starting our own little piece of family history.

The only problem is, this time we have to be the parents.

Firstly, it's the packing up of the car and, however much you share domestic arrangements with your other half, for some reason it is always the mum's job to pack for a holiday. Packing for yourself is one thing (I pride myself on having the capsule wardrobe thing down to a colour-coded art), but packing for your children when holidaying in the UK means trying to cover every possible eventuality. Clothes for sunshine, rain, mud, heat, cold, snow, beach, playground, walking, going out to a nice restaurant (pause for ridiculing laughter) or possible alien invasion must be included. Then you have to decide which books and toys they are going to take. Do you risk their current favourites knowing this will make them happy but jeopardising your future happiness should they be lost? Do you allow them to take everything that they want to or try and restrict them to just a couple of items? After all, as 'the mum' it will be your job to try to sneak Thomas the Tank Engine and his 17 friends into an already packed car whilst your husband swears and mutters something about 'it's a one week holiday, we're not bloody moving house'. Holidaying in the UK seems to turn men into their fathers, too.

Next item for debate, do you take food? Whilst we know that they do have supermarkets all over the UK, there is always the temptation to take 'something for breakfast tomorrow' or 'a few essentials to start us off' – five bags of shopping later and I have nowhere to put my feet when I get into the car. Snacks for the journey are a must. I spend at least 60% of the journey throwing sweets and crisps over my head in the hope that some of them hit the laps of the children behind.

One of the biggest differences for our children are the advent of car seats: an absolute necessity for car safety, but not half as much fun as making a duvet tent on the back seat and eating Smarties by torchlight. On the upside , we don't have to deal with two children kicking seven bells out of each other under a blanket whilst we shout, "Don't make me come back there!"

There have been many scientific advances in the last thirty years which make a long car journey easier on parents. Wet wipes, for example, are a huge improvement on my mum's damp flannel in a polythene bag which was as rough as sandpaper and smelt of sick. I also have no idea how parents coped on long journeys before the invention of the in-car DVD player or iPad. I've tried to play eye-spy with my children in a nostalgic nod to my car journeys of the '70s, but quite frankly it doesn't cut it when compared with Angry Birds on the iPad or Peppa Pig on DVD. These devices are no longer a luxury item for a long car journey with kids. Put it this way, I don't know any parents who have made the mistake of forgetting the in-car charger twice.

The fact that there is more traffic on the road now than there was then can also add to the stress of the journey. Encountering a traffic jam is never a pleasant experience but when you have two over-tired, sugar-fuelled children on the back seat, hitting traffic opens up a whole new world of pain. Also, this is usually the cue for the phrase that strikes panic into the heart of any travelling parent: "Mummy, I need the toilet."

After cajoling, distracting and begging the full-bladdered child in question for as long as it takes to get to a service station, it can be quite annoying when you do get there and suddenly the urgency seems to have subsided as the supposedly 'desperate' child takes their time, wandering past the games machines, having a look in the shop window, maybe even climbing onto the massage chair. Other users of the coffee lounge look at me askance as I scream, "Do you need to poo or not?"

The part that really makes me realise that I am now the mum is the very last leg of the journey. Whilst husband and I generally share the driving on a long car journey, as we approach our destination there is an unwritten rule, for the sake of our marriage, that husband drives and I navigate. This is because I need more warning to turn right than, "This right! This right! This right! . . . . Oh, you've missed it." Once, after a particularly horrendous Sat Nav re-routing, we found ourselves at 2am down a boggy track in Yorkshire, in torrential rain, having to reverse the car for about two miles. Even husband said it was the moment he wished his dad was there to do it instead.

When, with relief, you realise you have actually found your holiday destination, it dawns on you that the end is not yet in sight. Looking back at your sleeping children, you realise that, as the parents, it is up to you to locate the hidden key, work out how to open the door, make up the beds and carry your, hopefully still sleeping, children into bed. Then you have to go back outside and unpack the car, work out how to use the heating controls and check that you haven't forgotten the toilet paper, before you can finally make yourself a cup of tea and collapse onto the sofa.

Because that's what it means to be the parents on a holiday journey; you are the ones with whom the buck stops. It is as this sinks in, that I find myself awash with nostalgia for 1978, a sleeping bag on the back seat of a Ford Cortina and a wet flannel in a polythene bag.

Thanks Mum and Dad x

Supermarket Sweep

I know last time I took you,
I swore it would be the last.
But we've only two fish fingers left
and the bread has breathed its last.

Please stay in the trolley,
it really would be better.
I know you want to be helpful
and be mummy's little 'getters.'

But mummy's rather in a rush
to get this shopping done.
This is called a domestic chore,
it's not supposed to be fun.

Don't touch that tottering food display
and put back that DVD.
I know you have some money,
but they're more than 50p.

That lady does have funny hair
but please don't point like that.
And, no, we don't need cat food
as we haven't got a cat.

If you both behave yourself,
I'll buy you each a treat.
I was thinking just some stickers,
not a lifesize Happy Feet.

Until we've paid, it's stealing
if you start to eat a biscuit.
Oh sod it, yes just open them -
it's easier to risk it.

Yes I can see the woman
with the tiny little baby.
She's staring at you terrified,
of what's coming to her maybe.

It's rather hard to keep my calm
as people start to frown.
(Ironic you choose the frozen bit
to have a big meltdown.)

I want to kiss, mums that give me
'I've been there too' smiles.
And give us friendly knowing looks
as I belt around the aisles.

Trying to remember
what I must get from the Deli.
Really isn't helped much
by you crawling on your belly.

So NOW you want to get back in
and rest your weary legs?
You've squashed the lettuce, crushed the crisps
and sat down on the eggs.

Let's just go, we've got the bulk,
the rest of the list can keep.
No-one's been 'round here so fast
since Supermarket sweep.

Somehow we make it through the tills
and past the security men.
And I crawl towards the exit
crying, "Never, ever, again!"

Craftily Creative

A recent study from the University of Illinois suggests that drinking alcohol does in fact make you more creative. This may explain why doing craft activities with my children makes me want to lay down on the kitchen floor and drink gin from the bottle.

I do not have a creative bone in my body. I have friends who are able to take toilet rolls, cereal boxes and tissue paper and construct scale models of the Tower of London. I am able to take the same materials and turn them into life size models of . . . toilet rolls stuck onto cereal boxes.

I do try. I have a big plastic box full of sparkly pipe cleaners, tissue paper and stickers. Unfortunately, it appears that just buying the stuff is not enough; you then need to work out what to do with it.

Mr Maker is my freakin' nemesis. I try my best to turn my children away from the TV before he makes an appearance. Both my children worship him, watching his creations with hushed reverence. Unfortunately, as soon as he is finished they look at me with eyes full of eternal hope and (misplaced) parental belief: "Can you help us make that, mummy?"

If, by chance, we happen to have all the resources needed, I reluctantly agree to try. (Any attempts to get out of it by telling them that I'm not very good at making things only prompts the boy to hoist me with my own petard, "You won't get any better if you don't practice, mummy.")

Despite following the instructions meticulously, it never ends up looking as it should. Anyone who saw our dinosaur with legs made of rolled up newspaper would no longer question why they became extinct: the poor creature could only stay upright for about 3 seconds.

At least my children have obligingly low expectations. Although sometimes there is something more than a little patronising when a four year old tells you that you are "getting very good at cutting out."

My other sticking point, if you'll pardon the pun, is Mister Maker's obsession with 'googly eyes'. I'm pretty sure you'll find his brother is the UK distributor for the damn things. How the hell do you get them to stick to anything? Pritt stick (my non-spillable glue of choice) just doesn't cut it. If you use PVA they slide slowly downwards until the imaginary creature is looking out of its imaginary stomach. There is double-sided sticky tape, but if anyone out there has found a way to cut that small enough to fit a googly eye and still be able to peel the back off of the bugger, I will shake that person by the hand. (Actually, they do stick to something. I was in the middle of admonishing a Year 8 for their lack of effort in class when the confused looking child said 'Miss, why have you got eyes stuck to your buttons?' It's quite difficult to maintain your authority after that.)

Also, what the heck do you do with all these projects after you have made them? I used to get away with filing them in the recycling bin pretty soon after they were made (don't gasp in horror, supermothers, this blog is not for you) but lately they have taken to want to display them for indefinite periods of time. Sometimes I can get away with persuading them that that particular collection of painted pebble monsters would look lovely at Nana's house, but most of the time they are adamant that they want to litter my lounge with them. My latest plan is to implement a genius idea shared by a friend who takes a photo of the current masterpiece and then 'loses" the original. Now, that's the kind of creativity I can run with.

Back to that study from the University of Illinois: the researchers believe that 'intoxication may lower one's ability to control one's thoughts, thus freeing the mind for more creativity.' On reading further, however, they note that 'higher doses of alcohol were not tested, **nor was the study done with female volunteers**.'

Never let it be said that I would stand in the way of scientific progress. Or that I am unwilling to offer my services to further the advancement of the human race. Anyone else fancy joining me in a bit of research?

Dear Dad

You taught me how to ride a bike and how to tell a joke.
To make up before the sun went down and that promises mustn't be broke.
You taught me to be generous but also how to save.
You taught me books are precious things and showed me what was brave.

Not to sulk or bear a grudge, the importance of forgiving,
To never take a sickie and work hard to make a living.
That good friends and your family are the greatest kind of wealth.
(And that ever being rude to mum was dangerous for my health.)

And now as my own children grow, I wish that you were here.
With every milestone they achieve and more each passing year.
I wish that they could know you; I just wish that you were there.
I wonder what you'd think of them, my precious crazy pair?

But then I open up my mouth and it's your voice comes out.
When I tell them to 'breathe through your nose' or "I'm right here, don't shout!'
I hear you when I read to them (though my voice is not as deep.)
And I often use your Beatles songs to sing them off to sleep.

I make them laugh when they hurt themselves just as you would do.
The jokes I tell to make them smile were the ones I learned from you.
My arms that hold them, lips that kiss, were the ones you made for me
And sometimes in a smile, a frown, in them it's you I see.

And then I know that you are here, in everything I do.
In every word and thought and deed, your influence comes through.
And I smile and know that you're not gone, I still have what I had.
I'm the parent that I am today, because you were my Dad.

Dinner Guests

Next time I invite friends for Sunday lunch, I am going to ask my children to do the following.

When you see me opening and closing the oven door, whilst trying to select a flattering yet casual outfit and simultaneously throwing any stray toys/shoes/dirty plates into the cupboard under the stairs, I would like you to:

1. Find a food or drink that stains and spill it down yourself. Timing is key for this one, you must wait until you've just been changed into your 'nice' clothes. You may well be still in your pyjamas ten minutes before the guests arrive, but don't be tempted to do the spilling too early.
2. Tip a whole box of craft materials onto the floor of the kitchen, preferably the really small shiny stuff that it is impossible to vacuum or sweep up and must be picked up, individually, with fingertips.
3. Decide that you both want to play with the same toy and fight over it relentlessly. (Remember that this one is even more effective if the toy in question is a baby toy that you've just found behind the sofa and that neither of you has shown any interest in for the previous 12 months.)
4. When you tire of this, find a toy that has a million tiny pieces (jigsaw puzzles work well here, or any kind of play set which includes tiny figures) find that one piece is missing and cry/whinge until someone helps you to find it.

When the guests arrive:

1. Don't share any of your toys with the visiting children, particularly if the visiting child is asking you very nicely, with impeccable manners and offers to share their own toys in exchange.
2. Refuse to eat any dinner, demanding chicken nuggets or similar.
3. During dinner repeat "Why can't we watch a DVD while we have dinner like we usually do?" ad infinitum.

When they follow these instructions to the letter, I will be able to smile proudly, in the knowledge that I am an Alpha Mother whose children obey my every command. No longer will I be crying into the washing up that no-one listens to a word I say.

If, on the other hand, they revert to type and do the exact opposite of my requests, I will be able to relax and have a lovely afternoon as my guests look on in envy at my perfect children.

Either way, I win.

Dear Teacher

I know you're rather busy
First day back, there's just no time.
A whole new class of little ones
And this one here is mine.

I'm sure you have things covered
And have done this lots before.
But my boy is very little
He hasn't long turned four.

In his uniform this morning
He looked so tall and steady.
But now beside your great big school
I'm not quite sure he's ready.

Do you help them eat their lunch?
Are you quick to soothe their fears?
And if he falls and hurts his knee
Will someone dry his tears?

And what if no-one plays with him?
What if someone's mean?
What if two kids have a fight
And he's caught in between?

You're right, I have to leave now
It's time for him to go.
I'm sure he'll learn so much from you
Things that I don't know.

Yes, I'm sure they settle quickly
That he's fine now without me.
I know he has to go to school
It's just so fast, you see.

It seems like just a blink ago
I first held him in my arms.
It's been my job to love, to teach
To keep him safe from harm.

So, when I wave goodbye in a moment
And he turns to walk inside,
Forgive me if I crumple
Into tears of loss and pride.

I know as I give him one more kiss
And watch him walk away,
That he'll never again be wholly mine
As he was before today.

When the class toy comes home. . .

Parents of preschool and above aged children will be aware of the practice of sending a class mascot home with each child in turn, so that they can take pictures of him (Her? It?) and themselves with a little write up about what they did together. A lovely idea to bring together the worlds of home and school and something a lot of children love to do.

When the boy was at preschool, I was pathetically eager to have the school bear home on a visit. A lot more eager than my ambivalent son, who could barely remember the bear's name. (Edward, in case you're interested.)

Unfortunately, my plans for exciting and artistic shots of Edward having the time of his life were scuppered when the bear came home on a Wednesday. Wednesday being the day that daddy collected the boy from preschool.

Thursday evening, around 6:30pm, as we get the children into their pyjamas, husband says in passing, "Oh, I think we're supposed to take that bear back tomorrow."

Dramatic pause before I turn my head 180 degrees and ask, "WHAT bear?"

Husband, still unaware of his impending doom, continues, "You know, the bear they all take home. Edward, is it?"

Cue 45 minutes of me redressing the boy, dragging him outside with Edward bear (henceforth known as 'that bloody bear') to take photos of them bug hunting in the garden. Then, leaving husband to do bedtime (only the beginning of his penance), I quickly print the photos (lack of ink in the printer giving them a nice green tinge) and cut them out ready to stick in Edward's diary.

Thinking we may have gotten away with it, I open the book to be greeted with the previous entry. Four pages of meticulously written text which described how Edward has been to the fire station, ate out at a restaurant, had a ride on a motorbike . . . probably found time to scale Ben frickin' Nevis. No wonder the poor sod looked bored out of his brains at our house.

Now the boy is in reception at big school and apparently there's a new toy in town: Leo the bear has now commenced his home visits.

This time I am planning to tell the truth. Our entry into Leo's diary is likely to read something like this:

> *Leo watched TV for three hours with his friends William and Scarlett. He had chicken nuggets and chips for dinner. (No, make that homemade chicken goujons and potato wedges.) He then ran around the house for an hour brandishing light sabers and making unfunny jokes about poo before mummy had a mini-breakdown and sent them all to bed. Leo was then stuffed unceremoniously back into William's bag after mummy had taken a picture of him which she could later superimpose onto pictures of really exciting places.*

Because that's the kind of mother I am now. I don't need to impress anyone by pretending my weekends are full of exciting child-friendly activities that any bear would be lucky to be a part of. I am confident that I can show the world what our leisure time is really like. I will not be intimidated into competing with the adrenaline-fueled excitement which accompanies the visits of a small stuffed toy!

Yeah, who am I kidding? We're taking him to Hawaii.

Christmas Eve

T'was the night before Christmas
And all through the house
Not a creature was stirring
Not even my spouse.

I've wrestled the turkey
All the veggies are peeled,
There's just a few presents
Waiting to be sealed.

I've been buying since autumn
To fill up their sacks,
The pound shop's a wonder
For lots of cheap crap.

Colouring books, crayons
Thousands of stickers.
Bubble bath, funny socks
Bright Disney knickers.

As the clock goes past midnight
The last gift is wrapped.
And I count one more time
There's the same in both sacks.

Then I creep to their bedrooms
To check they're asleep.
'fore a sack full of presents
I rest at their feet.

Remembering that feeling
Of Christmas morns past.
When I'd wake in excitement
"He's been mum! At last!"

And despite all the headaches
The stress and the fuss,
I send thanks to heaven
That now it's for us.

To make for our small ones
The magic we had;
Once we were the children
But now mum and dad.

And I feel what an honour
We have this December,
To make Christmas memories
They'll always remember.

So leaving, I whisper,
As I turn out the light,
"Happy Christmas to all
And to all a good night."

Dear God

Whilst I appreciate that you have been in the business of creating human beings for a long time now, I would like to humbly suggest some modifications should you decide to revise the current version of small child.

1. Ear functionality - small child V1.0 seems to experience intermittent audio loss, otherwise known as selective hearing. This can vary between acute deafness and the hearing of a superhero i.e. an inability to hear the phrase 'Sit down and eat your dinner" whilst being able to hear the crinkling of a sweet wrapper from three rooms away. (NB Husband V2.0 could also benefit from this bug fix.)

2. A glitch in brain synapsis which renders an incomprehension of the word 'no'. This incomprehension manifests itself when the small child continues to repeat a question if it is answered with 'no'. As in:
"Can I have sweets before dinner?"
"No."
"Please can I have sweets?"
"No."
"Pleeeeease can I have sweets?"
This can continue through several cycles and often ends with an incessant whining sound and leakage from the eyes.

3. Lapses in memory. This takes two forms: inability to retrieve information (("I don't know where I left your purse after I was playing with it.") and general memory loss (" I forgot that I'm not allowed to help myself with biscuits from the cupboard.")

4. Shutdown malfunction. I have been reliably informed by several user manuals that you can program your small child to automatically shut down at a set time each evening. My model seems unable to perform this effectively and often requires me to perform the shutdown sequence several times. It also turns itself back on too early or at random times in the night. Also, the younger of my two models sometimes crashes mid-afternoon which makes the evening shutdown even more difficult.

I hope you are not offended with my suggestions to improve your otherwise excellent model; those of us in the field can often experience practical issues which may not have been considered important in the design phase. On that subject, there are a number of modifications which would greatly benefit Mother v2: an extra set of hands, larger reserves of patience and the ability to concurrently cook dinner, supervise a craft activity and negotiate a peace treaty to name but a few.

Otherwise, I am very happy with both of my small child V1.0 although I will not be purchasing further copies.

Yours humbly

Mrs A. Mother

IF (Inspired by Rudyard Kipling)

If you can keep your head when all about you
Is an ever growing pile of toys and games.
If you can referee a fight about a felt tip
And still love both the fighters just the same.
If you can function on three hours of sleeping
And still be running 'round the park next day.
If you can cook whilst helping out with homework
And listening to all they have to say.

If you can clean a room with just some wet wipes
And understand the cleaning up will never cease.
If you can bear to re-box mixed-up jigsaw puzzles
And stay up 'til you've found that final piece.
If you can thank them for the 'dinner' that they've made you
Even though the mess confirms your deepest fears.
Or watch the lounge that you've just tidied cluttered
And start again to tidy without tears

If you can make a fort with toilet rolls and Pritt stick
And cope with glitter stuck to all your clothes.
If you can sit through Kid's TV without a vodka
(even if you sometimes have a little doze.)
If you can keep all entertained on long car journeys
With puzzles, games and shrink wrapped healthy snacks.
And stay calm even though you feel like swearing
When World War Three still kicks off in the in the back.

If you can read the same book ten times over
Keeping perfectly to every word and rhyme.
If you can hear the same lame joke repeated
And laugh enthusiastically each time.
If you can listen to your children's constant moaning
Without going completely 'round the bend.
Yours is the pure love unconditional
And – which is more – you'll be a mum, my friend.

I was going to be . . .

I was going to be the parent who never raised her voice.
Who cooked you fresh organic food, bought only wooden toys.

Today I've screamed a thousand times and threatened measures drastic.
You've had chips, three times this week, and our lounge is full of plastic.

I was going to be the parent with a craft box fully stocked.
Tissue, card and googly eyes: a Pritt stick ready cocked.

But I found I couldn't make stuff; my creations were pathetic.
And glitter makes me want to drink until I'm paralytic.

I was going to be the parent who made your birthday cake.
But after one horrendous fail, I'm now a shop-bought fake.

I was going to be the parent who kept every childhood something.
But I seem to have lost your lock of hair and your baby book has nothing.

I planned on baby massage, baby yoga, all things artistic.
What you got was: 'baby watch whilst mummy eats her weight in biscuits.'

I thought I'd be the parent who loved her child a lot.
Kept them safe, fed them well and cleaned their stinky bot.

But the love I felt when you were born just knocked my off my feet.
A love that makes me place my hand just to feel your heart's soft beat.

I may not be the parent that I first set out to be.
But I'm the parent that truly loves you and forever that I'll be.

ABOUT THE AUTHOR

Emma Robinson writes the blog Motherhood for Slackers which takes a humorous look at motherhood. She also has a Facebook page for her poetry and short quips and anecdotes from family life.

Recently Emma wrote a poem entitled 'Dear Teacher . . ." which proved so popular she decided to write some more. She is also hoping to publish her first novel, about a group of first-time mothers, early 2015.

Emma is married to Daniel and they have two children, William aged 5 and Scarlett aged 3 who are much funnier than their parents. Emma is an English teacher and lives in Essex.

Follow Emma's Facebook page www.facebook.com/motherhoodforslackers or read her blog at www.motherhoodforslackers.blogspot.com

Printed in Great Britain
by Amazon.co.uk, Ltd.,
Marston Gate.